THE BACON BOOK

IT'S EXACTLY WHAT IT SOUNDS LIKE

BY
HEATH D. ALBERTS

DIGITAL NINJAS MEDIA, INC.

The Bacon Book: Published by Digital Ninjas Media, Inc. Printed in the United States of America. For further information, please address Digital Ninjas Media, Inc. [www.digitalninjasmedia.com).

Cover design by Heath D. Alberts
Author Photo by Diane Hill

ISBN-13: 979-8588332392

FIRST DIGITAL NINJAS MEDIA EDITION Published in The United States – 12/30/20
20 21 22 23 24 25 26 ❖ 10 9 8 7 6 5 4 3 2 1

Original Works by Heath D. Alberts

<u>Fiction</u>

Terminal Beginning
Last Rights
The Battery Man
Deeper
Photographic Memory
Not on the List
A Twist of Fate
The Meaning of Light
The Bacon Book
Rockford Writes (Contributor & Editor)
Forest City Stories (Contributor & Editor)
Dark Dreams & Weird Worlds (Contributor)
Interstellar Journeys (Contributor)
Temporal Journeys (Contributor)
Life Blood (Contributor)

<u>Non-Fiction</u>

Guerrilla Business
Guerrilla Business 2.0
Secret Rockford (Contributor)
Dave's Not Here (With Dave Block)
Love Me...Please? (With Dave Block)

The DNM Historic Revival Collection

<u>Young Adult Fiction</u>

The Sock Stories Omnibus
Cab & Caboose
The Boy Settlers

<u>Fiction</u>

Poems on Golf
The Loves of the Angels
Tamerlane & Other Poems

A Strange Manuscript Found in a Copper Cylinder
Tales of Terror
Hope Trueblood
The Pot Upon the Wheel
The Financier
Gadsby
The Haunted Bookshop
Against the Grain (À Rebours | Against Nature)
Flatland
Arms and the Man

<u>Non-Fiction</u>

Fasting for the Cure of Disease
The Great Book Collectors

Lincoln's Defense of Duff Armstrong
Anecdotal Lincoln
Abraham Lincoln: An Address
Abraham Lincoln: His Early Youth & Manhood With A Brief Account Of His Later Life
Victory Turned into Mourning: A Discourse on Occasion of the Death of Abraham Lincoln
Homicide, North and South
The Occult World
Pioneer History of the Champlain Valley
Primitive Secret Societies
Watching Spirits
Patience Worth: A Psychic Mystery
A Pickle for the Knowing Ones
The Woman Movement
Knut Hamsun
The Life & Adventures of Wilburn Waters
The Life & Adventures of Nat Foster
The Story of the Trapper
Two Years' Residence in the Settlement on the English Prairie

<u>The Revolutionary War</u>
The New Jersey Volunteers

<u>The Spanish-American War</u>
K Company: 71st Regiment, New York Volunteers
"Right Forward, Fours Right, March!"

<u>The Civil War</u>
Memoir of the Reverend Elijah P. Lovejoy
The Diary of Orville Hickman Browning
Army Life of an Illinois Soldier
The Dismissal of Major Granville O. Haller
The Cannoneer: Recollections of Service in the Army of the Potomac
Memorial of Pickering Dodge Allen
Leaves from the Diary of an Army Surgeon
Leaves from a Trooper's Diary
Nurse and Spy in the Union Army
The Soldier Boy's Diary Book
The Color Guard
The Fighting Quakers
Stone's River: The Turning-Point of the Civil War
The History of Company A, 2nd Illinois Cavalry
The Red Neck Ties: A History of the 15th New York Cavalry
History of the 23rd Pennsylvania Volunteer Infantry
A Brief History of the 69th Regiment Pennsylvania Veteran Volunteers
History of the 85th Regiment, Illinois Volunteer Infantry
New History of the 99th Indiana Infantry
A Brief History of the 100th Regiment Pennsylvania Infantry Veteran Volunteers (Roundheads)
Abraham Lincoln: An Address
Victory Turned into Mourning: A Discourse on Occasion of the Death of Abraham Lincoln

Visit www.heathdalberts.com for a complete & current list of titles on offer

"The remedy is worse than the disease."
- Francis Bacon

CHAPTER 1: BACON BEGINS

Bacon BACON BACON bacon bacon BACON bacon
bacon bacon bacon bacon bacon
BACON bacon bacon BACON bacon BACON bacon
bacon bacon bacon bacon bacon bacon bacon bacon bacon
BACON BACON BACON BACON BACON BACON BACON
BACON BACON BACON bacon BACON BACON BACON bacon
bacon BACON BACON bacon BACON BACON bacon
bacon bacon B A C O N BACON
BACON BACON BACON bacon bacon
BACON bacon bacon bacon BACON bacon
BACON BACON bacon BACON BACON bacon
BACON BACON bacon BACON bacon BACON baco
bacon BACON bacon BACON BACON BACON bacon
BACON bacon BACON bacon bacon bacon bacon bacon
bacon bacon bacon bacon BACON βacθη
bacon BACON bacon bacon bacon bacon BACON
BACON BACON BACON BACON BACON BACON bacon
bacon bacon bacon bacon bacon bacon bacon
bacon bacon bacon bacon bacon BACON bacon
BACON bacon BACON bacon bacon bacon bacon
bacon bacon BACON BACON BACON bacon
bacon BACON bacon bacon bacon bacon bacon
BACON bacon bacon bacon bacon bacon bacon
bacon bacon bacon bacon
B∠▱□∅ BACON bacon bacon BACON BACON
BACON bacon bacon bacon bacon bacon bacon bacon
BACON bacon bacon BACON bacon bacon bacon BACON

bacon BACON bacon bacon bacon bacon BACON
BACON BACON bacon BACON bacon BACON
BACON bacon bacon bacon bacon bacon
bacon bacon BACON bacon bacon BACON bacon BACON
bacon bacon bacon BACON bacon BACON BACON BACON
bacon bacon B A C O N bacon bacon BACON
BACON bacon BACON bacon bacon BACON BACON bacon
BACON BACON bacon BACON bacon BACON
bacon BACON bacon BACON bacon bacon bacon bacon
BACON con BACON bacon
BACON BACON bacon
BACON BACON BACON BACON BACON
BACON BACON BACON bacon BACON bacon
bacon bacon bacon bacon bacon bacon BACON
BACON BACON BACON bacon bacon BACON bacon
BACON bacon bacon BACON con bacon bacon bacon
BACON BACON bacon bacon bacon bacon bacon bacon
BACON BACON bacon bacon bacon bacon
BACON BACON BACON bacon bacon BACON BACON
bacon bacon bacon bacon bacon bacon bacon BACON
BACON bacon bacon BACON BACON BACON bacon
bacon bacon bacon bacon bacon BACON
BACON BACON bacon BACON bacon bacon
bacon BACON bacon bacon bacon bacon BACON bacon
bacon bacon bacon bacon bacon BACON bacon
bacon bacon BACON bacon bacon BACON BACON
bacon bacon bacon bacon bacon bacon bacon bacon bacon

bacon bacon bacon BACON bacon BACON bacon bacon

bacon bacon BACON bacon BACON bacon bacon

BACON BACON BACON bacon bacon bacon

bacon bacon bacon bacon bacon

BACON

BACON bacon bacon bacon bacon bacon

BACON bacon BACON BACON bacon BACON bacon bacon

bacon bacon BACON bacon bacon bacon bacon bacon

bacon BACON bacon bacon bacon bacon BACON

BACON BACON BACON bacon bacon bacon bacon

bacon bacon BACON bacon bacon bacon

BACON BACON BACON BACON

BACON bacon bacon BACON BACON bacon bacon

BACON bacon bacon BACON bacon bacon BACON

bacon bacon bacon bacon bacon

bacon bacon bacon BACON bacon bacon bacon bacon

BACON bacon BACON bacon BACON BACON bacon

BACON bacon bacon bacon BACON BACON

bacon bacon bacon BACON BACON bacon bacon

bacon bacon BACON BACON BACON bacon BACON

BACON bacon bacon BACON bacon BACON bacon bacon

bacon BACON bacon bacon BACON bacon

bacon BACON BACON bacon BACON bacon bacon

bacon bacon BACON bacon BACON bacon BACON

bacon BACON BACON bacon BACON bacon BACON

BACON bacon BACON bacon BACON bacon

BACON bacon BACON bacon bacon bacon bacon bacon
bacon bacon bacon bacon bacon bacon bacon BACON
bacon BACON bacon BACON bacon bacon bacon
bacon BACON bacon BACON bacon BACON bacon bacon
BACON BACON BACON BACON BACON
bacon BACON bacon BACON BACON bacon bacon bacon
bacon bacon bacon BACON BACON bacon BACON
BACON BACON BACON BACON bacon BACON bacon bacon
BACON bacon bacon BACON BACON BACON BACON
bacon bacon BACON bacon bacon bacon bacon bacon
bacon bacon bacon bacon bacon BACON bacon
BACON bacon bacon bacon bacon bacon bacon BACON
bacon bacon bacon bacon bacon bacon BACON
bacon bacon BACON bacon b a c o n bacon
bacon BACON bacon BACON bacon bacon bacon bacon
bacon Bacon BACON bacon bacon bacon BACON bacon
bacon BACON bacon bacon bacon BACON
BACON bacon bacon bacon BACON bacon
bacon BACON bacon bacon bacon bacon BACON BACON
bacon bacon bacon BACON bacon BACON bacon
BACON bacon bacon bacon BACON BACON
BACON bacon bacon BACON bacon BACON bacon bacon
bacon bacon BACON bacon BACON bacon BACON
bacon BACON BACON bacon bacon bacon bacon BACON
bacon bacon bacon BACON bacon bacon bacon bacon
BACON BACON bacon bacon BACON bacon BACON bacon
bacon bacon bacon BACON bacon BACON BACON bacon
bacon BACON bacon BACON BACON BACON bacon
BACON BACON bacon bacon BACON

BACON BACON BACON BACON bacon

BACON BACON BACON bacon bacon bacon bacon

bacon bacon bacon bacon BACON bacon BACON bacon

bacon bacon bacon bacon bacon bacon b a c o n bacon

bacon bacon bacon b a c o n bacon bacon bacon bacon

bacon bacon bacon bacon bacon bacon bacon BACON

BACON bacon bacon BACON BACON

BACON bacon bacon BACON bacon bacon bacon BACON

BACON bacon BACON bacon bacon b a c o n bacon BACON

BACON BACON BACON bacon BACON BACON bacon BACON

BACON BACON BACON BACON bacon bacon bacon

bacon bacon bacon bacon bacon BACON BACON

bacon bacon bacon bacon bacon_bacon bacon BACON

bacon BACON bacon bacon bacon BACON

BACON bacon bacon BACON BACON

BACON bacon bacon bacon bacon BACON bacon

bacon bacon bacon BACON bacon BACON BACOn

bacon bacon bacon bacon ®©©||% bacon bacon bacon

BACON bacon BACON bacon BACON bacon

BACON bacon bacon bacon bacon bacon bacon bacon

bacon BACON bacon BAC°N bacon BACON bacon bacon

bacon bacon bacon BACON bacon bacon bacon bacon

bacon BACON bacon BACON bacon bacon BACON

bacon BACON BACON bacon bacon BACON

bacon bacon BACON BACON BACON bacon

bacon bacon bacon bacon bacon BACON BACON bacon

bacon bacon BACON bacon

BACON bacon_bacon bacon bacon bacon bacon BACON

bacon BACON bacon b a c o n bacon

bacon bacon bacon bacon bacon BACON

bacon BACON BACON BACON bacon bacon bacon BACON

bacon BACON bacon BACON [illegible] BACON bacon

bacon BACON bacon bacon bacon BACON bacon bacon

BACON bacon BACON BACON bacon bACON BACON

BACON bacon bacon BACON bacon BACON bacon BACON bacon

BACON BACON bacon BACON bacon BACON BACON

BACON BACON BACON bacon BACON bacon

[illegible] BACON bacon BACON BACON

BACON BACON BACON bacon BACON BACON bacon

ckchclsksh BACON bacon bacon bacon bacon bacon

BACON BACAN BACON bacon BACON BACON

BACON bacon BACON BACON bacon bacon bacon

BACON bacon BACON bacon BACON bacon BACON

bacon BACON BACON bacon bacon bacon bacon BACON

bacon bacon bacon bacon BACON bacon bacon bacon

BACON bacon BACON bacon bacon BACON bacon

bacon BACON bacon BACON BACON bacon BACON

BACON bacon bacon BACON BACON bacon BACON bacon

BACON bacon bacon BACON BACON බඅචඔන bacon

bacon bacon bacon bacon BACON bacon BACON bacon

BACON bacon bacon bacon BACON bacon BACON bac BACON

bacon BACON bacon bacon bacon BACON BACON BACON

bacon bacon BACON BACON BACON BACON

BACON BACAN bacon BACON bacon bacon bacon bacon

bacon bacon BACON bacon bacon bacon bacon

bacon BACON bacon bacon BAGON bacon bacon bacon

BACON BACON bacon BACON BACON

CHAPTER 2: BACON II: ELECTRIC BOOGALOO

Bacon bacon bacon bacon BACON bacon BACON
bacon bacon BACON bacon bacon bacon BACON BACON
bacon BACON BACON BACON bacon BACON BACON
bacon bacon bacon bacon bacon bacon bacon
bacon bacon BACON bacon bacon bacon
bacon BACON bacon bacon BACON bacon
bacon bacon bacon bacon bacon bacon bacon
BACON bacon BACON bacon bacon bacon
BACON BACON bacon bacon BACON B4CON
BACON bacon BACON bacon bacon
BACON BACON bacon BACON B4CON
bacon bacon BACON BACON bacon BACON bacon
BACON bacon bacon bacon bacon bacon BACON
bacon bacon BACON BACON
BACON B4CON BACON BACON BACON bacon
bacon bacon BACON bacon bacon BACON BACON bacon
BACON BACON BACON bacon BACON BACON
bacon bacon bacon BACON BACON BACON
bacon bacon bacon BACON BACON BACON
bacon bacon bacon bacon BACON bacon
BACON BACON bacon BACON bacon bacon BACON
bacon BACON BACON BACON BACON bacon bacon
BACON bacon bacon bacon bacon BACON bacon
BACON bacon bacon BACON
bacon bacon bacon BACON BACON bacon BACON BACON bacon
BACON BACON BACON bacon BACON

BACON bacon bacon BACON bacon bacon BACON
bacon bacon bacon bacon BACON bacon bacon bacon
bacon bacon BACON bacon bacon bacon BACON bacon
bacon bacon bacon bacon BACON BACON BACON
BACON bacon bacon BACON BACON BACON bacon
bacon bacon bacon bacon bacon bacon bacon bacon
bacon bacon bacon bacon bacon bacon BACON
BACON bacon bacon bacon BACON bacon BACON BACON
bacon BACON [illegible] bacon bachon bacon bacon BACON
bacon bacon bacon bacon bacon bacon bacon bacon
BACON bacon b'acon BACON bacon baçön BACON
BACON BACON BACON bacon BACON bacon bacon
bacon bacon BACON BACON [illegible]
bacon bacon bacon bacon BACON bacon [illegible]
bacon bacon [illegible] bacon BACON bacon ACON
bacon bacon bacon bacon bacon bacon BACON
BACON bacon BACON BACON bacon BACON
bacon BACON BACON BACON [illegible] bacon bacon bacon
bacon bacon bacon BACON bacon bacon bacon
bacon bacon bacon bacon bacon BACON bacon bacon
BACON BACON [illegible] BACON bacon BACON
bacon bacon bacon bacon bacon bacon bacon bacon BACON
bacon BACON bacon bacon bacon bacon bacon bacon bacon bacon
bacon bacon bacon bacon bacon BACON bacon BACON
BACON bacon bacon bacon bacon bacon
BACON bacon bacon bacon BACON bacon bacon bacon
bacon bacon BACON BACON baron bacon bacon

bacon BACON bacon BACON bacon BACON BACON

bacon bacon bacon BACON bacon bacon bacon BACON

BACON bacon BACON bacon bacon bacon

bacon BACON bacon βαχον BACON BACON bacon

BACON bacon BACON BACON bacon bacon bacon bacon

BACON bacon BACON bacon bacon BACON bacon bacon

BACON bacon BACON BACON BACON bacon BACON

bacon bacon BACON bacon bacon BACON BACON

bacon bacon bacon BACON BACON bacon bacon bacon

BACON BACON ◊◊◊◊◊ BACON BACON BACON bacon

BACON bacN°N° bacon bacon bacon bacon

bacon bacon bacon BACON BACON bacon bacon BACON

bacon bacon bacon BACON bacon bacon bacon bacon

bacon BACON bacon bacon BACON bacon bacon bacon BACON

BACON BACON bacon BACON BACON bacon bacon

bacon bacon bacon BACON BACON bacon

bacon bacon bacon BACON bacon BACON BACON BACON

bacon bacon bacon BACON bacon bacon bacon

BACON BACON bacon bacon bacon BACOD bacon bacon

bacoo BACON bacon bacon bacon BACON bacon

BACON bacon bacon bacon BACUN bacon bacon めむもつん

bacon bacon bacon bacon bacon BACON bacon bacon

BACÖN bacon BACON BACON BACON bacon BACON

BACON bacon bacon BACON

BACON BACON bacon bacon bacon BACON BACON

bacon BACON bacon BACON bacon BACON BACON

bacon BACON bacon BACON bacon bacon BACON bacon bacon

bacon BACON bacon BACON bacon BACON acon

BACON bacon BACON bacon bacon BACON

bacon BACON bacon bacon BACON BACON bacon

BACON BACON bacon BACON bacon BACON

BaCON BACON BACON bacon BACON bacon

bacon BACON bacon bacon bacon bacon BACON

bacon BACON bacon bacon bacon BACON

BACON bacon bacon bacon bacon bacon bacon

BACON BACON BACON bacon bacon bacon

bacon bacon BACON bacon bacon bacon bacon

bacon ba-ON BACON bacon bacon BACON

bacon bacon bacon BACON BACON

BACON bacon BACON bacon bacon BACON

bacon BACON BACON bacon bacon bacon

BACON BACON bacon bacon bacon bacon bacon

bacon bacon BACON BACON bacon bacon bacon bacon

bacon bacon BACON BACON bacon bacon BACON

BAGON BACON bacon bacon bacon bacon

BACON bacon bacon bacon bacon bacon BACON BACON

BACON bacon bacon BACON bacon bacon

BACON bacon bacon BACON BACON bacon bacon

BACON BACON BACON BASON BACON bacon

BACON bacon bacon BACON bacon bacon bacon

bacon bacon bacon bacon BACON bacon

bacon bacon BACON bacon bacon bacon

BACON BACON BACON bacon

CHAPTER 3: BACON BITS

Bacon bacon bacon BA<ON BACON bacon bacon BACON
bacon bacon b con bacon bacon BACON BACON
bacon BACON BACON bacon bacon bacon bacon bacon
bacon BACON BACON bacon bacon bacon bacon bacon
bacon BACON bacon bacon bacon bacon bacon
bacon BACON bacon bacon bacon bacon bacon
BACON BACON bacon bacon BACON BACON bacon BACON
bacon bacon bacon BACON bacon BACON BACON BACON BACON
bacon bacon BACON BACON BACON bacon
bacon BACON bacon BACON BACON bacon bacon bacon
bacon BACON bacon bacon bacon BACON bacon bacon
bacon bacon bacon bacon bacon bacon bacon
bacon BACON bacon BACON bacon bacon bacon
BACON bacon BACON bacon bacon bacon bacon BACON
bacon bacon bacon BACON bacon bacon BACON bacon bacon
bacon BACON bacon BACON BACON BACON bacon
BACON bacon bacon bacon BACON bacon bacon
BACON Bacon BACON BACON BACON bacon bacon
bacon BACON bacon BACON BACON BACON bacon
bacon bacon bacon bacon BACON bacon bacon bacON
bacon BACON bacon BACON BACON bacon bacon BACON
BACON bacon BACON bacon BACON bacon bacon bacon
bacon bacon BACON bacon bacon BACON
BACON bacon bacon BACON BACON bacon
bacon bacon bacon bacon bacon bacon BACON bacon
BACON bacon BACON BACON bacon bacon BACON bacon

bacon bacon BACON bacon BACON BACON bacon
bacon BACON BACON BACON bacon
bacon BACON bacon bacon BACON BACON bacon
bacon bacon bacon bacon BACON bacon bacon
BACON BACON bacon BACON bacon bacon
BACON BACON BACON BACON bacon BACON
bacon bacon bacon bacon bacon bacon BACON bacon
bacon bacon BACON bacon BACON BACON BACoN
BACON bacon BACON bacon BACON bacon bacon BACON
bacon bacon bacon bacon bacon BACON bacon bacon bacon bacon bacon
BACON bacon bacon BACON bacon bacon bacon BACON
bacon BACON bacon bacon bacon BACON
BACON bacon bacon bacon bacon bacon bacon
bacon BACON BACON bacon bacon bacon bacon bacon
bacon BACON bacon bacon bacon BACON
bacon BACON BACON BACON BACON bacon bacon bacon
bacon bacon bacon bacon bacon BACON BACON BACON
bacon BACON bacon bacon BACON BACON BACON
bacon bacon bacon BACON bacon BACON bacon BACON
bacon BACON bacon BACON BACON bacon BACON
bacon BACON BACON BACON BACon BACON
bacon BACON bacon bacon BACON BACON
BACON bacon BACON bacon BACON BACON
BACON bacon BACON BACON BACON bacon bacon bacon
BACON bacon bacon BACON BACON BACON bacon bacon
BACON bacon bacon bacon BACON BACON BACON bacon
bacon BACON bacon bacon bacon bacon bacon bacon bacon
bacon bacon BACON bacon bacon bacon BACON BACON
BACON BACON bacon bacon bacon BACON bacon

bacon bacon bacon BACON bacon bacon bacon bacon
BACON bacon BACON BACON BACON BACON BACON
bacon bacon bacon BACON bacon BACON BACON bacon
Bacon bacon BACON bacon bacon bacon bacon bacon
BACON bacon BACON bacon bacon bacon BACON Bacon
bacon bacon BACON bacon BACON BACON
bacon bacon bacon bacon bacon bacon BACON bacon bacon
bacon BACON BACON BACON
bacon bacon bacon bacon bacon bacon BACON bacon
bacon bacon bacon bacon bacon bacon bacon bacon
↕↦⇕◦□ BACON bacon BACON bacon BACON bacon
BACON BACON BACON bacon BACON
BACON BACON BACON bacon bacon bacon BACON
□□□500.5 bacon bacon bacon □□□□□ bacon BACON BACON
bacon BACON bacon BACON bacon BACON BACON
BACON bacon BACON bacon BACON bacon BACON bacon
BACON bacon BACON BACON BACON bacon bacon
bacon bacon bacon bacon bacon bacon bacon
BACON BACON BACON bacon BACON bacon bacon
bacon BACON BACON BACON bacon
bacon BACON bacon BACON bacon BACON bacon bacon
BACON bacon bacon bacon BACON BACON BACON bacon BACON
bbbbb bacon BACON bacon BACON BACON BACON
BACON BACON BACON bacon bacon bacon bacon
BACON BACON BACON bacon BACON bacon bacon bacon
BACON bacon bacon bacon bacon bacon BACON
BACON BACON bacon bacon bacon BACON

bacon bacon bacon bacon BACON BACON BACON

bacon BACON bacon bacon BACON bacon BACON JVUAR

bacon bacon BACON bacon bacon bacon bacon

bacon BACON BACON bacon bacon bacon

bacon bacon BACON BACON bacon BACON

BACON BACON bacon bacon BACON bacon bacon

BACON bacon bacon bacon bacon bacon bacon bacon BACON

bacon bacon BACON BACON BACON bacon bacon

BACON bacon bacon BACON bacon bacon BACON

bacon bacon BACON BACON bacon BACON

b a c o n bacon bacon bacon bacon BACON bacon bacon

BACON bacon bacon BACON BACON BACON bacon BACON

bacon bacon bacon bacon bacon BACON bacon

BACON bacon BACON bacon bacon BACON bacon

BACON BACON bacon BACON bacon BACON bacon

BACON bacon bacon bacon bacon bacon bacon

bacon BACON BACON bacon bacon bacon bacon bacon BACON

bacon BACON bacon BACON bacon BACON bacon BACON

BACON BACON BACON bacon bacon BACON BACON

BACON bacon bacon bacon bacon bacon bacon bacon

bacon bacon bacon BACON BACON BACON BACON BACON

bacon bacon bacon bacon BACON BACON BACON BACON

BACON BACON bacon BACON BACON BACON bacon

bacon bacon BACON BACON bacon bacon BACON BACON

BACON BACON BACON bacon bacon bacon bacon

bacon bacon BACON bacon bacon BACON BACON

BACON bacon BACON BACON bacon bacon bacon

BACON bacon bacon bacon bacon BACON BACON BACON

bacon BACON BACON bacon BACON bacon BACON

BACON bacon BACON BACON bacon bacon
BACON BACON BACON BACON bacon bacon
bacon bacon bacon bacon bacon bacon
bacon BACON bacon BACON BACON bacon bacOn
BACON BACON bacon BACON BACON bacon
BACON bacon BACON BACON bacon bacon BACON BACON bacon
BACON BACON BACON bacon bacon BACON BACON BACON
BACON BACON bacon BACON BACON bacon
bacon BACON bacon BaCON BACON bacon bacon
bacon bacon BACON bacon bacon bacon bacon BACON
bacon BACON bacon BACON bacon bacon bacon bacon
bacon bacon BACON bacon bacon bacon
bacon BACON bacon bacon bacon BACON BACON bacon
bacon bacon bacon BACON bacon bacon
BACON bacon BACON BACON BACON
BACON BACON BACON BACON bacon
BACON bacon BACON bacon BACON BACON BACON bacon
BACON bacon bacon bacon BACON bacon BACON bacon
BACON ✓♦✓on bacon bäcon BACON BACON BACON BACON
BACON bacon BACON BACON bacon bacon BACON
B A C O N bacon bacon BACON bacon bacon
bacon bacon BACON BACAN bacon KACON
bacon bacon bacon BACON bacon bacon bacon bacon
bacon bacon BACOM BACON bacon bacon bacon bacon
BACON BACON bacon bacon BACON BACON
Bacon bacon bacon bacon bacon bacon
BACEN bacon bacon bacon
BACON BACON bacon B A C O N bacon bacon BACOO
bacon BACON BACON BACON bacon BACON bacon bacon

BACON bacon bacon bacon BACON bacon BACON bacon
bacon bacon BACON BACON BACON bacon bacon
BACON bacon bacon Bacon bacon bacon BACON
bacon BACON bacon bacon bacon BACON bacon bacon
BACON bacon bacon bacon bacon BACON bacon BACON
BACON bacon BACON BACON bacon BACON bacon bacon
bacon BACON bacon bacon bacon BACON BACON
BACON BACON bacon bacon bacon BACON bacon BACON
bacon BACON BACON Bacon bacon BACON BACON BACON
BACON bacon BACON bacon BACON bacon bacon
bacon bacon bacon BACON bacon bacon BACON bacon
BACON bacon BACON bacon BACON bacon BACON bacon
bacon BACON BACON bacon bacon BACON bacon
bacon BACON BACON bacon bacon bacon BACON
BACON bacon Bacon bacon bacon bacon bacon BACON BACON
bacon BACON BACON BACON bacon BACON BACON bacon
BACON BACON BACON bacon bacon bacon BACON
bacon bacon BACON bacon bacon bacon bacon
BACON bacon bacon bacon bacon bacon bacon
bacon bacon BACON bacon bacon bacon BACON BACON
BACON BACON bacon BACON BACON BACON bacon
BACON bacon BACON BACON BACON BACON bacon bacon
bacon bacon BACON bacon bacon bacon BACON
bacon bacon bacon bacon BACON bacon
BACON BACON bacon bacon BACON BACON BACON
BACON bacon bacon BACON BACON bacon bacon BACON
BACON bacon BACON bacon BACON bacon bacon BACON

CHAPTER 4: NO FAKIN' - WE'RE MAKIN' BACON!

bacon bacon BACON BACON BACON bacon
BACON BACON BACON bacon bacon bacon
bacon bacon bacon BACON bacon BACON BACON
BACON BACON bacon bacon BACON bacon
BACON bacon bacon bacon BACON bacon bacon
bacon BACON BACON bacon BACON
bacon bacon BACON BACON bacon BACON BACON
BACON bacon bacon BACON BACON bacon bacon
BACON BACON bacon BACON BACON bacon bacon
bacon bacon BACON bacon bacon bacon bacon bacon
BACON BACON bacon bacon BACON bacon
BACON BACON BACON bacon BACON bacon
bacon bacon bacon bacon bacon BACON bacon bacon
BACON BACON bacon BACON БДСФИ BACON bacon
bacon BACON bacon bacon bacon bacon BACON bacon
bacon bacon BACON bacon BACON BACON bacon bacon
bacon bacon BACON bacon bacon bacon bacon bacon bacon
BACON BACON BACON bacon BACON bacon bacon bacon
bacon bacon bacon bacon bacon bacon bacon BACON
bacon BACON BACON BACON bacon BACON bacon
BACON bacon bacon bacon BACON bacon bacon
B A C O N bacon BACON BACON bacon bacon
bacon bacon bacon BACON bacon BACON BaCoN
bacon bacon BACON bacon BACON bacon BACON
bacon bacon BACON bacon bacon BACON bacon bacon
bacon BACON bacon bacon AC bacon
BACON bacon bacon bacon bacon bacon bacon

bacon bacon BACON bacon BACON bacon bacon BACON

BACON bacon bacon BACON bacon bacon BACON BACON

BACON bacon BACON bacon bacon bacon bacon

BACON BACON BACON bacon BACON bacon bacon

BACON bacon BACON bacon bacon

bacon bacon bacon BACON bacon bacon bacon bacon

BACON bacon bacon BACON bacon bacon BACON bacon bacon

BACON bacon bacon bacon BACON bacon BACON bacon

bacon bacon bacon bacon bacon bacon bacon bacon BACON bacon

BACON bacon bacon bacon bACON BACON bacon

BACON bacon bacon bacon bacon bacon BACON

bacon BACON bacon BACON bacon BACON BACON

bacon bacon BACON bacon bacon bacon bacon

bacon bacon bacon bacon bacon BACON bacon bacon

bacon bacon bacon bacon bacon bacon BACON bacon bacon

bacon bacon bacon BACON BACON bacon bacon

bacon bacon BACON bacon BACON

bacon bacon bacon BACON bacon bacon bacon bacon

bacon bacon bacon bacon BACON bacon BACON

BACON bacon bacon bacon bacon BACON bacon bacon

BACON bacon bacon bacon BACON bacon bacon bacon

BACON bacon BACON BACON bacon

bacon bacon bacon bacon bacon BACON

bacon bacon bacon BACON bacon BACON

bacon BACON bacon bacon bacon bacon BACON bacon

bacon bacon bacon bacon bacon bacon bacon bacon

bacon bacon bacon bacon βαχον

bacon BACON bacon bacon bacon bacon BACON bacon BACON
BACON bacon bacon bacon bacon BACON
bacon bacon bacon bacon bacon BACON bacon

BACON bacon bacon bacon BACON bacon ↓←∂(∑

bacon bacon BACON ベーコン BACON bacon bacon

BACON BACON bacon bacon 𝄢 𝄞 bacon BACON bacon
bacon bacon bacon bacon bacon bacon BACON

bacon ✔ □ ▲ ● BACON bacon bacon BACON bacon
bacon BACON BACON bacon bacon ♌♋♍□■ BACON
bacon BACON bacon bacon bacon bacon bacon
bacon BACON bacon ⇦⇨⇨⇕⇔ bacon
⑥⑤ BACON BACON bacon BACON bacon bacon
BACON 培根 .

THE END

ABOUT THE TYPEFACE

There's no way in Hell I'm looking into the origins of all of these thousands and thousands of fonts. So, let me summarize by saying: A lot of people (and possibly robots?) brought all of these fonts to life. Vanity or hubris was involved on some levels, on some occasions, probably. Also...aliens?

www.ingramcontent.com/pod-product-compliance
Lightning Source LLC
Chambersburg PA
CBHW061327140726
47998CB00007B/2583

* 9 7 9 8 5 8 8 3 3 2 3 9 2 *